All about...

Anne Fine

Vic Parker

www.heinemann.co.uk/library

Visit our website to find out more information about **Heinemann Library** books.

To order:
☎ Phone 44 (0) 1865 888066
▤ Send a fax to 44 (0) 1865 314091
▯ Visit the Heinemann Bookshop at www.heinemann.co.uk/library to browse our catalogue and order online.

First published in Great Britain by Heinemann Library, Halley Court, Jordan Hill, Oxford OX2 8EJ, part of Harcourt Education. Heinemann is a registered trademark of Harcourt Education Ltd.

Editorial: Lucy Thunder and Helen Cannons
Design: David Poole and Geoff Ward
Picture Research: Rebecca Sodergren and Kay Altwegg
Production: Edward Moore

Originated by Repro Multi-Warna
Printed and bound in China by South China Printing Company
The paper used to print this book comes from sustainable resources.

ISBN 0 431 17987 5 (hardback)
08 07 06 05 04
10 9 8 7 6 5 4 3 2 1

ISBN 0 431 17997 2 (paperback)
09 08 07 06 05
10 9 8 7 6 5 4 3 2 1

British Library Cataloguing in Publication Data
Parker, Vic
All about Anne Fine
823.9'14
A full catalogue record for this book is available from the British Library.

Acknowledgements
The Publishers would like to thank the following for permission to reproduce photographs:
BBC p**21**; John Cleare pp**10**, **14**; Collections p**8**; Egmont Books Limited p**15**; Anne Fine pp**5**, **6**, **7**, **9**, **12**, **13**, **16**, **18**, **22**, **23**, **25**, **28**, **29**; Chris Honeywell p**4**; Jacqueline Howard / Corbis Sygma p**20**; Robbie Jack / Corbis p**27**; Macmillan Publishers Ltd p**11**; Penguin Books Ltd p**26**; Tudor Photography p**19**.

Cover photograph of Anne Fine winning the Whitbread Book Award 1996, reproduced with permission of PA Photos.

Sources
The author and Publishers gratefully acknowledge the publications which were used for research and as written sources for this book:

An Interview With Anne Fine
(Egmont Books, 2002)
Teacher Support Network website – www.teacherline.org.uk **12**
Anne's own website – www.annefine.co.uk **18**
Stories from the Web website – www.storiesfromtheweb.org **19**
Tiscali website – www.tiscali.co.uk **22**, **25**
The *Guardian's* learning website – www.learn.co.uk **28**

Fiction works by Anne Fine are cited in the text.

Contents

Any words appearing in the text in bold, **like this**, are explained in the glossary.

The author and Publishers would like to thank Anne Fine for her invaluable help in the writing of this book.

Who is Anne Fine?

Anne Fine is one of the most popular children's authors today. She is famous all over the world for books such as *Goggle-Eyes*, *Flour Babies*, *Madame Doubtfire* and *Bill's New Frock* among many others. Her stories have been translated into over 25 languages and turned into films, TV programmes and plays. Anne writes for all age groups and has won every major award for children's books – some of them twice! In 2001 Anne was given the special title 'Children's Laureate'. This is an honour awarded once every two years to an outstanding writer or **illustrator** for children. Anne was the second person ever to have won it.

What are Anne's stories about?

Anne writes about issues that affect families – from big problems like **divorce** to smaller arguments, such as those about keeping a pet. Both children and adults love her work because she sees both kids' and grown-ups' points of view.

▲ Anne has written many books for all ages. Here are some of them.

A true bookworm

Anne has strong opinions about book **publishing** and is known for being very outspoken. For instance, Anne does not agree with many people who think that the cover of a book is important. She says that the picture on the front should not matter a bit because it is the words inside which make the story enjoyable or not!

Anne has such strong opinions because, ever since she was tiny, her greatest pleasure has been books. She is passionate about reading. Anne says: 'Everyone needs books. The more you read, the richer you are inside...'

▲ Anne, the world-famous author.

Factfile

★ Date of birth	7 December 1947
★ Star sign	Sagittarius
★ Eye colour	Blue
★ Hair colour	Mousy grey
★ Pets	A big hairy dog called Henry
★ Hobbies	Reading, walking
★ Favourite food	Toasted cheese
★ Favourite childhood book	*The Once and Future King* by T. H. White
★ Bad habit	Biting my nails
★ Personal motto	'Sufficient unto the day is the evil thereof' (which means 'there are enough things to worry about today, so don't go worring about tomorrow too'!)

Early years

Anne's parents, Brian and Mary, met and got married during **World War II**. The couple settled in Leicester and had their first child, a baby girl, in 1944. Anne was their second child, born three years later, after the war had finished.

Brian and Mary would have liked a son, but the next baby turned out to be triplets – and all girls! So Anne grew up as one of five sisters. As a child, her favourite fairy tale was *The Twelve Dancing Princesses*, because the family had only girls, just like her own.

◀ Anne's father and mother walking in a park in 1952.

The pressures of parenting

Anne's mother must have found it extremely hard work to look after five young children. Anne's stories often involve parents who are under pressure in different ways, such as dealing with divorce in *Madame Doubtfire*. In *Flour Babies*, a class of children is given the chance to find out about the strains of parenthood for themselves when they are given 3-kg (6-lb) bags of flour to look after like real babies.

Starting school

When Anne was a toddler, the family moved to the seaside town of Fareham, in Hampshire. The family lived next door to a school, Highlands Road Infants School. The school took Anne two years early, to give her mother more time to look after the triplets. So Anne was very young when she learned to read. From then on, she was hooked on books and loved nothing better than to spend hours reading. Anne spent an extra year at Highlands, because she was ahead of her age group. Sometimes, she repeated work she had done before. Other times, she was allowed to borrow any book she liked from the head teacher's office and read instead. Anne thought that was fantastic.

▲ Anne as a toddler, with her mother in 1949.

Anne at play

Anne loved being outdoors. She often played outside in the garden, or went off exploring with a small gang of kids from nearby houses. (In those days, children were much freer to do things by themselves than nowadays.)

▲ Anne and her family loved playing on the beaches in Hampshire, like this one.

Sometimes Anne's family all piled into the car and her father drove them to one of the pebbly beaches not far from their home. Anne thought it was great to roam about on the shore all day and has loved the sea ever since.

On wet days, Anne could most often be found in a quiet corner indoors lost in a book. She also enjoyed making little storybooks for all of her toys by doing 'scribble writing' on scraps of paper and sewing them together.

A new school

Anne went to Wallisdean Primary School from the age of seven. Besides the usual lessons, Anne did country dancing, nature walks, gymnastics, singing, swimming and violin lessons. She enjoyed performing in school plays, and learning poetry and folk songs – many of which she can still remember to this day!

Anne's favourite teacher was Mr Simpson. She thought his lessons were great. He encouraged Anne and her classmates to use their imagination by reading them *The Hobbit*. He also played them recordings of stories set to music, such as *Tubby the Tuba* and *Peter and the Wolf*.

▲ Anne (right) played the Wicked Witch in *Sleeping Beauty* at school in 1954.

What Anne says

The class Anne enjoyed most was Composition (writing). The teacher jotted some titles on the blackboard, then everyone chose one and wrote a story, working in silence.

'I loved those double lessons more than anything in the world (except for reading). No endless discussions. No sharing of ideas ... I covered reams of paper. I wrote fast. And I learned to judge the form and the length of a story. It was the best training I could ever have had, though I didn't know I'd be a writer...'

A library child

When Anne was eight, her family moved to a house that overlooked a graveyard. For months Anne was terrified. She was sure that her bedroom was haunted! Every night, a glowing skull shape appeared on her bedroom wall. It turned out to be made by the landing light shining through the keyhole of Anne's bedroom door!

Anne was much happier when her family moved again, a couple of years later, to a big old house in the countryside in Northamptonshire. She often spent whole days mucking about in lanes and woods and fields with two best friends. The house itself had a beautiful walled garden, and Anne used to climb into an apple tree and sit there for hours, munching on the fruit and reading and reading and reading…

▲ Anne spent many hours walking and playing in the country lanes of Northamptonshire.

Ideas from real life

Anne never forgot the glowing skull shape that she had seen on the wall as a child. Many years later she turned the scary experience into a story: *The Haunting of Pip Parker*.

Living at the library

When Anne was not reading, she was usually on her way to the library for more books. The rule was only two books at a time, yet Anne used to get through them in just a couple of days and go back again to swap them. One nasty librarian often did not believe that Anne had finished a book so quickly and told her to take it away again and read it properly!

Anne's first favourite author was Enid Blyton. She loved *The Magic Faraway Tree* and *The Famous Five*. As she grew older, she couldn't get enough of popular stories about boys, such as the *Jennings* books and the *Just William* stories.

Anne has said, 'You only get one chance to read a book first at the perfect age...'

She feels she was given **classics** too young, which put her off them. So she did not read many of the best children's stories, such as *The Phoenix and the Carpet* by E. Nesbit, until she was grown up.

▲ The mischievous *William* was one of Anne's favourite childhood storybook **characters**.

The bookworm at secondary school

Anne spent her teenage years at Northampton High School for Girls, where she was very happy. She disliked maths and science subjects, but enjoyed history, French, Spanish and, most of all, English. However, although Anne was passionate about reading and books, she never thought about the possibility of becoming a writer. When people asked Anne what she was going to do when she left school, she said what many girls did in those days: 'teacher' or 'librarian'. Sometimes Anne answered '**physiotherapist**', although she had no idea what a physiotherapist was!

What Anne's teacher said

A teacher once wrote on Anne's school report:

'*She may lack initiative – but I wouldn't know because she is always busy reading.*'

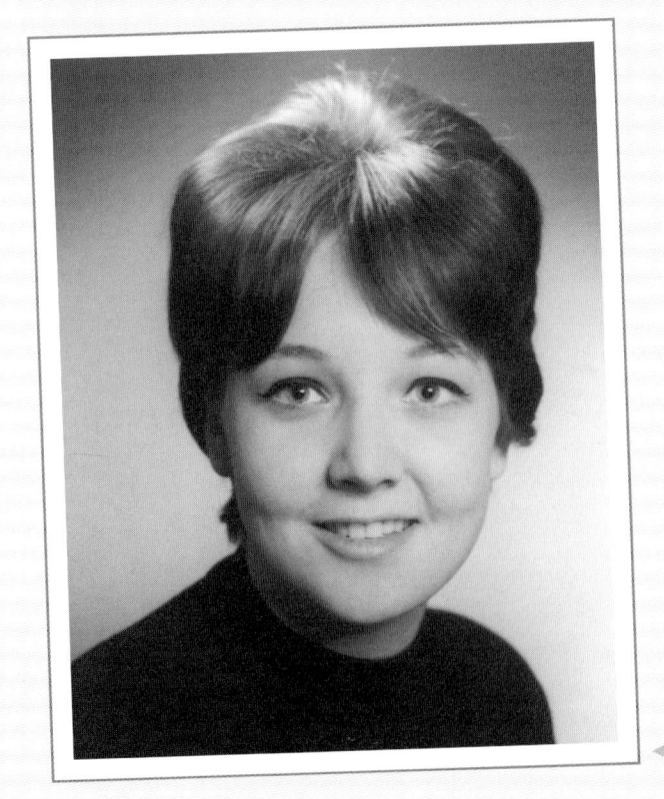

This is Anne's first passport photograph, taken when she was sixteen years old.

Anne becomes a writer

After leaving school, Anne studied History and Politics for three years at Warwick University. She fell in love with a teacher there called Kit Fine and, in 1968, they got married and settled near Coventry. Anne, who was now twenty, began working as a History and English teacher in a secondary school. However, she did not enjoy teaching much.

A year later, she was glad to give it up so that she and Kit could move to Oxford, where Kit had been offered a job at the university. Anne did a secretarial course and worked first for the **County Public Health Office**, then for a **charity** called Oxfam. Like nearly all young women in those days, Anne did not expect to have a big, important career because most girls gave up work when they had babies. Anne had always wanted children and she was overjoyed when her first daughter, Ione, came along in 1971.

▲ Anne and Kit on a weekend away.

Putting pen to paper

When Ione was just six weeks old, the family moved north to Edinburgh in Scotland, where Kit had a new job. Anne did some work teaching young people in a prison, but for most of the time she was stuck with her tiny baby in a freezing cold top-floor flat, a long way from all her family and friends. Anne grew very unhappy. The only thing that kept her going was visiting the library every day for more precious books.

One day there was a terrible snowstorm and Anne was trapped indoors with nothing to read. In desperation, she picked up a pencil and began to write.

Anne and Kit moved to Edinburgh, Scotland's capital city, in 1971.

Third time lucky!

Many authors work on story after story before they become good writers. However, Anne had not done very much writing at all before. When she was about twelve, she and a friend wrote a long tale called *Agatha the Witch*. Then, when Anne was 21 and living in Oxford, she wrote a story in her spare time. However, it was not long enough to be a proper novel for grown-ups. But in Scotland, Anne found that the words flowed quickly and easily. She says that it seemed as if the story wrote itself.

Success!

Anne wrote a light-hearted **novel** for older children about a girl called Ione, like her daughter. She called it *The Summer House Loon* and sent it to a couple of **publishers** to see if it could be made into a book. However, it was turned down. Anne was so disappointed that she shoved the story under the bed for a long time.

Then one day she noticed a newspaper competition for new writers. Anne was about to move to the USA for Kit's work. Hurriedly, she dusted off her story and left it with a friend to send in. To Anne's surprise and delight, the story won second place in the competition.

The winning story, *Thunder and Lightnings*, was by Jan Mark. Like Anne, Jan has since become a top children's author for all ages, and has also won the Carnegie Medal twice. As a result of the competition, Anne's story was finally published. At last, she had a book with her own name on it!

This is the cover of Anne's first book, *The Summer House Loon*.

Finding fame and fortune

The year 1975 was a fantastic one for Anne. She was not only runner-up in the writing competition, but she also gave birth to her second daughter, Cordelia. Over the next seven years, Kit's work took the family to California, Arizona and Michigan in the USA. Meanwhile, Anne continued writing.

Anne had fallen in love with her **characters** in *The Summer House Loon*, so the next book she wrote was another story about them – *The Other Darker Ned*. Then Anne wrote two more books for the same age group: *The Stone Menagerie* and *Round Behind the Ice-House*. They were all **published** by companies back home in the UK.

▲ Kit, Ione and Cordelia during a recorder session, at home in Edinburgh.

Returning to her roots

Anne began to feel that to write more children's books, she needed to live where she knew about children. This was of course the UK, where she had spent her own childhood. However, both Anne and Kit knew that it was best for him to stay in the USA, where his work was going well. In 1981 they made the difficult decision to separate. Anne returned to England with her daughters and started to balance being a single mum with a writing career.

The very first book Anne wrote upon returning to England, *The Granny Project*, was **shortlisted** in 1984 for a prize called the Guardian Children's Fiction Award. From that moment on, Anne's writing went from strength to strength. *Madame Doubtfire* was a storming success. It was shortlisted in 1987 for the Whitbread Children's **Novel** Award and was runner-up for the Guardian award.

An especially skilful storyteller

In *Madame Doubtfire*, the mother, Miranda Hilliard, is a successful businesswoman. The father, Daniel, is the opposite to Miranda – a fun-loving, out-of-work actor. The three children behave more like grown-ups than Daniel, trying to make him behave responsibly. However, Anne is well aware that people are not simply sensible or silly, boring or fun. For instance, Daniel usually criticizes Miranda, but when he is in disguise as the nanny, he sees her point of view and sticks up for her:

'Madame Doubtfire ... raised an imposingly large hand for silence. Turning to Christopher, she asked him gravely, "Young man, is that the way that you usually speak to your mother?"'

▲ Anne is shown here speaking after winning the Carnegie Medal for *Flour Babies*. The actor Michael Palin is standing to her right.

Anne began to write hugely popular stories for younger age groups, too. And she continued to win award after award. In 1990 *Goggle-Eyes* won both the Guardian award and the Carnegie Medal. *Bill's New Frock* won the 1990 Smarties Award and raced off bookshop shelves. In 1993 *Flour Babies* won both the Carnegie and Whitbread awards. In 1996 Anne won the Whitbread again for *The Tulip Touch*, which was also 'Highly Commended' for the Carnegie in 1997.

What the critics say

Every time one of Anne's stories is published, the **critics** shower it with praise.

'*Anne Fine's books are a true delight to read*'
        (Children's Fiction Sourcebook)

'*A remarkable writer*' (The British Book News)

'*This author is too much of a treasure to be reserved for children*'
        (The Independent)

'I bought Charm School for my younger sister aged eight as a Christmas present. She read it in under three hours and told me it was brill ... I started reading the book and before I knew it I was finished. I think it is really fab – and I am a boy!'

(Johnny, aged 15, from Denmark)

Fans of all ages

Anne is one of few authors who can write well for all age groups. She feels that the craft of writing involves working out the right age group for an idea and deciding on how to write about it. For instance, would the tale be told best as a picture book, a story book, a longer book for older readers with just a few pictures, or a wordy novel?

To date, Anne has written over 40 books for children of different ages and five novels for grown-ups. However, she prefers writing for kids rather than adults because she thinks that children are the keenest readers! Nowadays, Anne's books sell millions of copies all over the world. She has become one of the most popular writers for children ever.

▲ Anne has written over 40 books for children and her books fill many bookshops' shelves.

A hit for Hollywood

In 1993 *Madame Doubtfire* was made into a Hollywood movie. You might think Anne was thrilled, but in fact she was frustrated. Anne says 'books are best' because books can tell you what people think, whereas films and TV can only show you what people do and say. Anne prefers to have her books read on the radio, so the words of her stories are not lost, rather than having them turned into films or TV programmes.

▲ Robin Williams starred as *Mrs Doubtfire* in the film of Anne's book.

Keeping it real

Anne often writes to explore subjects that are bothering her. She wrote *Madame Doubtfire* and *Goggle-Eyes* because she was thinking about how **divorce** and remarriage affect families. A lot of readers sent her letters saying that real life was often not as simple as the happy ending in *Goggle-Eyes*. So Anne wrote *Step by Wicked Step* to look further at being part of a second family. In this book, a group of children on a school trip tell about their very different experiences of step-parents.

Having ideas...

Anne always keeps on the alert for spotting ideas. She might overhear an interesting conversation, or read about or see something unusual. For instance, *Countdown* was sparked off by a letter Anne saw in a newspaper about keeping animals in cages. The idea for *Bill's New Frock* began when Anne saw how girls and boys were treated differently at her daughters' primary school.

Anne jots down ideas and keeps them so she does not forget. Later, when she is ready to write, she imagines that she is a young reader and tells the story to herself. She says: 'I always end up with the kind of book I would have loved to read if only someone else had bothered to write it for me.'

▲ Anne's book *Goggle-Eyes* was made into a TV series in 1992/3. The series starred Honeysuckle Weeks, shown here, as Kitty.

The successful author

Today, Anne lives in a very old house in the countryside of County Durham, miles from anywhere. She shares her home with her partner, Dick, and their dog, Henry – and her grown-up children and step-children often drop in to stay for the weekend. Besides working on fantastic stories, Anne frequently spends her days at meetings, giving interviews and on visits to schools and bookshops. From time to time, she also goes on book tours to other countries all over the world.

▲ Anne entertains her fans at a book reading.

The best writers are often people who like spending time on their own, and who prefer writing to talking. However, the more famous an author is, the more people expect them to give talks and appear at events like book signings. Anne once said:

'I do think having the author do their own publicity is a bit of a waste. Secretly, I have always thought a sensible move would have been to invite my sister, who loves hotels and loves people, to have taken on the role 25 years ago. Then I would have written more books...'

A typical day in the life of Anne Fine...

On writing days, Anne usually wakes up about 7 a.m. Dick brings her a cup of tea and she reads the papers in bed. Then Anne takes Henry for a walk. Anne always has breakfast, as she cannot work well if she has not eaten. Next, she opens her post and deals with any urgent letters. Then she gets down to her writing.

Anne works right through lunchtime, munching on a sandwich at her desk. She gets tired around 4 p.m., so she might take Henry for another walk or soak in the bath with a good book, or round off the day by attending to the business side of writing: emailing her **editors**, sorting out travel arrangements, or answering invitations. Anne also writes replies to as many of her readers' letters as she can manage. However, it is not possible to write back to everyone as she receives enormous sackfuls of letters every week!

▲ Anne's dog, Henry.

Fans always ask Anne what they should do to become a writer like her. This is her advice:

'Read, read, read! Look after the reading and the writing will take care of itself later, because for some reason the practice for writing is not writing, but reading.'

The writer at work

Anne can work anywhere, as long as it is absolutely quiet so she can lose herself in the silence. She usually sits at a desk in the corner of her bedroom, looking out on a river and the sky. Anne uses a soft pencil, rubbing out and rewriting over and over again. As a child, she used to hate correcting her work, but now she finds it hugely satisfying. When Anne is happy with a section, she types it up on an old computer her daughter used at university. Then her work suddenly looks more like a book and Anne sees it in a new way, so she begins making changes all over again. A chapter has to be perfect before she will move on to the next one. Anne always keeps a copy of her work in the car, so if the house burns down she will not lose what she has written.

The right time to write

Many people say that they would love to write a book but they simply have not got the time. Anne always keeps a pad and pencil by the side of her bed in case she wakes up early in the morning. She finds she can write very well then, before the phone or the post disturbs her. She also confesses that she saves time for writing by rarely tidying up and only going shopping for essentials!

Getting from start to finish

Anne does not write for set hours or for a set number of words every day. She only writes when she is in the mood for it – but this is often. When she begins a book, she has strong ideas for the setting, and the main **character**, but she does not know how the story will go. Anne feels as though it already exists somewhere and she has to find it, rather than write it. She tries various things, such as starting from a different place in the tale or writing from a new character's point of view, until she has discovered how the story is meant to be. Anne has learned to be patient and not to give up, especially if she gets stuck. A **novel** for older children can take a whole year. She says that the fantastic feeling of finishing a book is the best part of the job.

▲ Anne spends many hours working at her desk, but only when she is in the right mood!

Anne Fine on Anne Fine

Here are some of Anne's answers to questions we asked her:

What is your house like?
'It's 200 years old, built of stone, and has a beautiful walled garden. Inside it has wooden floors covered by tattered old rugs, with shabby furniture from junk shops or given to me by friends. I hate shopping with all my heart, so I never throw anything away until it breaks.'

Do you collect anything?
'There are an awful lot of books in my house, but I don't collect them as such. I just keep books that I especially like and give others away to Oxfam.'

What do you do to relax?
'Reading, reading and more reading! I also love going to the cinema, but the nearest one is about 35 miles away.'

Out of all the books she has ▶ written, *Round Behind the Ice-House* is Anne's favourite.

▲ Anne loves the idea of being an opera singer, like the people in this picture, but admits she cannot sing!

Do you read books for children or grown-ups?
'I mostly go for new **novels** for adults, the **classics**, crime stories, poetry and books about the lives of famous people or the workings of the mind. I don't take enough holidays, but when I do, I adore being able to read totally uninterrupted by the phone or things to do.'

Out of all the books you have written, which is your favourite?
'*Round Behind the Ice-House* – although it doesn't seem to be anyone else's favourite!'

What would you have been if you hadn't been a writer?
'I would have loved to have been an opera singer, but I can't sing at all! Being realistic, I expect I would have made a good **publisher** or publisher's reader.'

Anne's future ambitions

Anne's wish for the future is not just to continue writing brilliant stories. She is determined to spread the enjoyment of reading to as many children round the world as possible.

The Children's Laureate

On 16 May 2001, Anne was given the special honour of being titled 'Children's Laureate'. This is a role awarded once every two years to a top writer or **illustrator** of children's books, to celebrate their outstanding work. As part of the job, Anne thought up a wonderful plan to make reading even more fun for everyone. She set up a website (www.myhomelibrary.org) with

hundreds of **bookplates** on it. The bookplates are designed by fantastic illustrators such as Quentin Blake, Nick Sharratt and Helen Oxenbury and you can print them out.

Anne hoped this would encourage children to own and read more books. They would not need to buy new books – many great books can be found in **charity** shops and at jumble sales. To Anne's delight, children all over the world now have bookshelves sagging with wonderful stories.

▲ Anne pictured at the launch of the magazine *Author Zone* in 2001.

▲ Anne visits many places to do readings, like this one at a library in Leeds. Anne is in the back row, left.

Watch this space!

Anne has plenty more ideas for new stories and cannot imagine there will ever be a time when she will want to give up writing. Besides, she has one particular ambition she is burning to achieve. She says: 'I would love to be the first person to win the Carnegie Medal three times! The Carnegie is the award that means the most to me because it is given by the Library Association. Without libraries, I would not have become a writer.' Surely it will only be a matter of time...

What the readers say

Children all over the world love Anne's books.

' . . . highly entertaining and enjoyable . . . '
　　　　(Sarah, aged 11, from the Vale of Glamorgan, Wales)

' . . . gets the reader thinking and involved . . . '
　　　　(Anna, from Iowa, USA)

'Awesome!'
　　　　(Serina, aged 12, from Melbourne, Australia)

Timeline

1947 Anne is born

1968 Marries Kit Fine

1971 First daughter, Ione, is born

1974 Goes to live in the USA

1975 Runner-up in Kestrel/Guardian competition for unpublished writers

Second daughter, Cordelia, is born

1978 Anne's first **novel**, *The Summer House Loon*, is **published**

1981 Anne returns to England with her daughters

1984 *The Granny Project* is **shortlisted** for the Guardian Children's Fiction Award

2001 Anne is appointed Children's Laureate

Books by Anne Fine

Here are some books by Anne you might like to read:

Madame Doubtfire (Hamish Hamilton, 1987)
When a divorced mother advertises for a cleaning lady, she unknowingly gives the job to her ex-husband in disguise!

Bill's New Frock (Methuen Young books, 1989)
A boy wakes up one morning to find he's turned into a girl!

Goggle-Eyes (Hamish Hamilton, 1989)
Kitty can't stand her mother's new boyfriend…

The Tulip Touch (Hamish Hamilton, 1996)
Natalie's friendship with the outlandish Tulip is exciting, but then Tulip's pranks start going too far…

If you would like to stay in touch with up-to-date news about Anne Fine and her work, you can log on to: www.annefine.co.uk

Glossary

bookplate decorative sticker that you stick in the front of a book and write your name on so everyone knows it is yours

character person in a story

charity organization that exists to help people rather than to make money

classics books that people always think are good, no matter how many years or fashions come and go

County Public Health Office local government department set up to check that public places (including restaurants and factories) are clean and safe

critic person whose job is to read a story (or see a film or other entertainment) and write their opinion of it

divorce legal process that people who are married go through to end their marriage

editor person in a publishing company whose job is to work with an author to make their story as good as possible

illustrator artist who draws pictures to go with the story or information in a book. Some authors illustrate their own books.

novel long story for older readers

physiotherapist person whose job is to give injured people special exercises and treatment to make them fit again

publish to produce and sell books. A company that publishes books is called a publisher. A published writer is one whose books are sold in shops.

shortlist to narrow a list of competitors down into a 'short list' (just a few names) from which the winner is picked

World War II war that lasted from 1939 to 1945. It began when Germany marched its army into Poland.

Index